"*Some books need to be Tasted, others to be Swallowed, and some few to be Chewed and Digested; that is, some books are to be read only in Parts; others to be read but not Curiously; and some few to be read wholly, and with Diligence and Attention.*"

-*Francis Bacon*

MINDING YOUR OWN BUSINESS*

FRANK BENDITT

*The practical guide
for new business owners.

This is a copy of the original work
published in 1989.
Reprinted with permission.

Dedication

I dedicate this book to my wife Susanne, my daughter Michelle and my son Frank, who provide me with my energy.

I am grateful to my previous employers and to the many men and women who are and have been my clients and also my teachers.

ABOUT THE AUTHOR

FRANK BENDITT, successful and prosperous entrepreneur of the 1980's, has established himself among the entrepreneurial elite with a multi-million dollar business enterprise which has been a profitable success for over seven straight years.

In 1981, Mr. Benditt composed a comprehensive new business plan, resigned his corporate managerial position, took a pay cut and assumed the role of Co-Owner, Chief Operating Executive and Secretary/Treasurer of Benditt & Hall Marketing, Inc. He later severed ties with his partner to form Benditt Marketing, Inc.

Under Mr. Benditt's guidance, these operations have grossed over fifteen million dollars in income by consulting and supplying leading American companies such as General Mills, IBM, Coca-Cola, Citicorp, Marriott and a major U.S. hamburger restaurant chain with effective business building concepts.

The recipient of various awards and citations while employed by a succession of U.S. corporations listed on the New York Stock

Exchange, Mr. Benditt has had an excellent corporate business career as well.

In addition to serving in project administration at one of our government's major defense contractors and working as an executive for a top-ten American advertising agency on a Fortune 500 account, he has also managed national advertising and sales promotion for a multi-billion dollar U.S. corporation represented in the Dow Jones industrial average.

Presented here is a practical guide designed for entrepreneurs and professionals who are already underway managing young privately-owned service, manufacturing or retail operations. In this informative work, the author shares his keen insight through personal observation of eight important areas which can often make the difference between business success and business failure within the first five years.

Contents

FORWARD

May 16, 2016

By Julius C. Dorsey, Jr.
President, Dorsey & Company,
Strategic Consultants to Management

Time tells the tale. So, I have no doubts whatsoever when I say the value of the lessons shared in Frank Benditt's 1989 book, Minding Your Own Business, are impossible to overstate. Since 1976, my work with Frank and opportunity to look in on his many accomplishments has been my most satisfying and valuable business experience. This vantage point also put me in the catbird seat to see these lessons learned, refined, and shared in this volume and then successfully applied by Frank and many others.

It should be a comfort to new entrepreneurs and seasoned executives alike; when reading this book again for the first time since 1989, I found immediate applications for myself and for clients we counsel. Not lofty, not pretentious, just clearly, cleanly and simply stated. Grasping the principles in Minding Your Own Business and seeing their role in improving operating results is instinctive for all who read with an open mind and sincere desire to do better. Those who apply these principles will enjoy the comfort of a foundation for their businesses that will support the growth and dynamic challenges that lie ahead.

Frank's book is full of truth, facts, and principles that seem common, but are rarely applied as more profound avenues to competitive advantage are sought. No matter how precisely the way to success is charted it rests on a foundation that cannot be overlooked or left to manage itself. Time doesn't change the truth.

"And so castles made of sand slips (sic) into the sea, eventually."

\- Jimi Hendrix, 1967

1

LUCK,
FORTUNE
AND
OPPORTUNITY

CHAPTER ONE

LUCK, FORTUNE AND OPPORTUNITY

"Luck to your young ambition, that is the way to the stars."
-Virgil

Congratulations! You have decided to strike out on your own during one of the most exciting periods in the history of American business. The decade of the 1980's has often been referred to by business writers and journalists as the "Era of the Entrepreneur." Most prominent business schools now offer courses in "Entrepreneurship" and many well-respected management consultants even advocate generating what is being called an "intrepreneurial" spirit among corporate executives and division managers within large organizations.

Whether you are running a start-up manufacturing company, managing a young professional service firm or operating a newly opened retail establishment, you can be absolutely certain of one definite fact…

You Are Not Alone!

Statistics recently published by the National Federation of Independent Business indicate American small business is growing by more than a half-million enterprises each year. People from all walks of life are starting up new business ventures these days. Professionals, housewives, executives, craftsmen, widows, artists, service technicians, hobbyists, students, you name it.

Approximately one-half million copies of *How to Form Your Own Corporation Without a Lawyer* by Ted Nicholas have been sold.

Starting and Managing s Small Business of Your Own has become one of the most popular booklets offered for sale by the Superintendent of Documents at the U.S. Government Printing Office.

Popular and best-selling books such as *Take a Chance to be First: The Secret of Entrepreneurial Success* by Warren Avis, Peter F. Drucker's *Innovation and Entrepreneurship*, and *Going For It* by Remington Razor chief Victor (the man who bought the company) Kiam, have influenced, inspired and encouraged those of us at this time who possess the desire to be our own boss, captain our own ship, start our own business.

Dun & Bradstreet Corporation, the New York financial information service, reported more than 700,000 new-business incorporations in 1986 alone, plus 250,000 unincorporated business starts, the overwhelming majority of them small entrepreneurial companies.

Today across America, thousands of new business enterprises are being started each and every day. At this astonishing rate, more men and women are seizing the *opportunity* to seek their *fortune* by starting a small business of their own than currently live in the cities of Chicago, Los Angeles, Boston, Detroit, Philadelphia, San Francisco or Washington, D.C. The number of American citizens joining the ranks of enthusiastic and hopeful entrepreneurs in this decade will exceed the combined total of all those joining the U.S. Army, Navy, Air Force and Marines each year. During the 1980's, more individuals will invest their hard-earned money in opening a new business venture than will purchase life insurance.

TIME Magazine's recent "Salute to Small Business" reports that small business alone creates three-fifths of all new jobs in the United States and provides one-half of the Gross National Product. As a world economic power, American small business ranks as the fourth largest economic force on earth, behind the U.S. as a whole, the Soviet Union and Japan. Ahead of England! Ahead of China! On the *upside*, the American free enterprise system has thrived in the 1980's.

On the *down side*, however, only half of all new business owners who have recently struck out on their own in an attempt to found a new business will advance their company from the *start-up* category to the *growth* position in the business cycle. The other half will not even last five years.

During the same month as the TIME Magazine small business feature appeared, USA TODAY published additional information shedding light on the *down side* of the environment which you have chosen for yourself by recently starting a new service, retail, manufacturing or professional business of your own. America's national newspaper reported that approximately one-third of all new business firms fail after one year. After four years, the failure rate approaches fifty percent (50%). Fully one-half of all new companies go out of business within their first five years. Only one in two recently founded commercial operations will make it past the *five year barrier*, recognized by many in business as the first real measure of long-term success. Of all who try, only half will succeed and half will fail.

With well over one-half million men and women striking out on their own each year, washout rates of this magnitude stipulate a grim prediction. Not only will millions of commercial enterprises founded during the 1980's fail to survive into the 1990's, but most of these failures have yet to occur. At these rates, approximately one-half million up and running business ventures founded within the past three years will cease to exist in the next three years. A drop-out rate of one business every 3 ½ minutes.

Another half-million establishments, which will be opened between now and 1990, will also go out of business.

Why will so many hard-working individuals, including many highly-trained professionals and successful corporate executives, who possess the motivation, drive and initiative to start their own companies, fail to make it in the long run? The answer is pure and simple: *money*.

When a business runs out of *money* it closes. Any enterprise which continuously fails to make a profit over time will eventually be driven out of business. But lack of profit is not the underlying reason why many new companies fail.

In fact, even a profitable company can run out of *money* and be forced to close its doors. (This paradox is covered in the next chapter). Business endeavors of all types fail for many and varied reasons. Even though many business decisions involve finance (*money*), running your own operation entails making many judgments concerning a wide range of business variables and evolving or dissolving depending on the consequences of your actions.

The number of American business failures started in this decade alone will exceed the total number of U. S. casualties suffered as a result of the Revolutionary War, War of 1812, Mexican War, Civil War, Spanish American War, World War I, World War II, the Korean War and Vietnam combined.

The failure rate does not have to be this high. Although competition in the American marketplace is keen, our expanding economy bears witness to the fact that it is not always competitive pressures which cause the failure of so many young, privately-owned companies.

Oftentimes, conscious internal business decisions deliberately and intentionally made by business owners get their companies into trouble and eventually lead to their demise. It is up to you to prevent your firm, company or organization from falling casualty to today's staggering failure statistics.

If 50% of all new business endeavors succeed and 50% are discontinued, in less than five years, what distinguishes success from failure?

Luck?

Since the odds of staying in business for five years are fifty-fifty, should we all just flip a coin and be done with it? Of course not. Over the years I've witnessed time and time again how luck is seldom the fickle lady she is often pictured as being. She seems more likely to bestow her favors on the deserving rather than the undeserving and she is especially apt to smile on entrepreneurs who work hard at minding their own business.

I once heard luck described as preparation colliding with *opportunity*. Although it is important in the success of any business to be ready when *opportunity* knocks, it is more important to open the door and look out once in a while. I know of one industrious entrepreneur who went bankrupt and then became successful selling seminars on corporate failure. How's that for opening the door to *opportunity*?

In the book, *A Kick in the Seat of the Pants*, Roger von Oech comments about the distinction between errors of commission which you make when trying something new and errors of omission which you make by doing nothing and perhaps losing an *opportunity*. Sometimes, von Oech says, the person who doesn't do anything and therefore doesn't make any mistakes is actually worse than the person who tries a few things and makes some mistakes. 1

Edison knew 1800 ways how <u>not</u> to make a lightbulb. One of Madame Curie's failures was radium. Columbus thought he had discovered the East Indies. Freud had several big failures before he devised psychoanalysis. Alexander Graham Bell's diligent work to invent a hearing aid, led to the discovery of the principles for the telephone.

The ideas presented in this book are conceptual

tools, made to be used, which takes effort, self-discipline and concentration. They form a conceptual framework designed to examine the assumptions underlying all of your business decisions. Minding Your Own Business is a concept much wider in scope than simply managing your new business. To *manage* is to get along in handling matters, but to *mind* is to attend to matters more closely and to be aware of the many and varied everyday misunderstandings which can get your business into trouble.

Application of this concept on an ongoing basis can help you to be among the one in two new business owners who succeed in reaching escape velocity and breaking the *five year barrier*.

The future of American small business may well be more prolific and the field more crowded tomorrow than it is today. According to Ernest

L. Boyer, President of the Carnegie Foundation for the Advancement of Teaching, in his 1986 study titled *College: The Undergraduate Experience in America*, between 1986 and 1990 there will be 12 million to 13 million jobs for some 15 million baccalaureate earners. 2

Success can certainly bring you *fortune* and the decisions you make today may well determine whether tomorrow you'll be singing "Bye Bye Business," or "Hello *Opportunity*. It's up to you. Good *luck*.

"A man must make his opportunity, as oft as find it"
          -Francis Bacon

2

MONEY, NUMBERS AND PROFIT

CHAPTER TWO

MONEY, NUMBERS AND PROFIT

"What would life be without arithmetic, but a scene of horrors."
-Sidney Smith

Now that you are your own boss, running your own business and having to meet expenses every month, you are highly familiar with the importance of what British author Robert Heller writes while describing his ten truths of management in the English version of his fine book, *The Naked Manager*, "The essence of *money* in management is, first, that cash in must exceed cash out."[1] The above appears to be a fairly straight-forward, easily understood statement. Many who consider this knowledge common among business managers may pass over it lightly or even dismiss this warning outright, but many new and profitable businesses fail every year because their owners violate this simple rule.

If you wonder how in the world someone entrusted with minding his or own profitable business could not be aware of a cash problem until it is too late, consider the difference in meaning of the terms *money, number* and *profit*.

Money is defined in common everyday terms as something generally accepted as a medium of exchange or means of payment. *Profit* is the excess of revenue over expenditures. *Numbers* are units of measure within a mathematical system. Yet, often these separate and distinct terms lose their individual identity and their elemental meanings are somehow transposed in the minds of many new business owners. This failure to differentiate *money* from *numbers* and *profit* has been and will continue to be one of the principal reasons otherwise seemingly successful privately-owned companies go under.

All business of any type is measured by *numbers*. Size is measured by assets, value by net worth and relative success is measured by *profit*. Each of these measurements is expressed by a *number* generated through an arithmetic process termed Accounting, which can sometimes complicate their interpretation. Though based solely on the simple mathematical functions of addition, subtraction, multiplication and division, the terminology and format of Accounting can often contribute to serious misunderstanding by the new business operator.

Now do not get me wrong. I have nothing against accountants in particular or the practice of Accounting in general. But most of us operating our own retail, manufacturing or service organization (except for CPA's) have developed particular entrepreneurial or professional skills other than the practice of Accounting. Those new business man and women who fail to consult with a knowledgeable professional accountant or CPA regarding financial decisions affecting their business before they take any action, will be the ones who get their companies into trouble by failing to recognize the difference between *money*, *numbers* and *profit*.

In his moving and insightful book, *Going For It*, Harvard Business School graduate and Remington Razor Chief Victor Kiam has this sharp bit of advice, "If you're going to be an entrepreneur in a corporation, or on your own, you should get a background in accounting. This may seem a small detail, but it's something I recommend to everyone no matter what his age." 2

Collegiate textbook authors William W. Pyle and John Arch White provide us with the following formal definition. "Accounting is the art of recording and summarizing business transactions and of interpreting their effects on the affairs and activities of an economic unit. 3

I advise you at this point not to overlook the dual nature of this definition. It is essential to realize that a complete understanding of the value of Accounting not only involves a working knowledge of how the various numerical measurements are calculated, but more importantly, the proper interpretation of what the numbers mean and what effect they have or will have on your new business.

Therefore, while relying heavily on standard accounting methods to supply data as information input concerning various business decisions, the operator of a young company who is not aware of Accounting's dual nature can be mislead and compound further his or her confusion regarding *money, numbers* and *profit*.

For example, many newly established manufacturing companies and professional service firms utilize the accrual method of accounting. Since this method allows your firm to book income before it is collected and charge expenses before they are paid, it is often the undoing of many extremely talented business entrepreneurs. They fail to realize that under the accrual accounting method, virtually every *number* that appears on their companies' operating income statements are only that, just *numbers*. You must be careful not to be led astray and confuse these *numbers* with *money* in any way, simply because the practice of accounting allows us to precede these *numbers* with dollar signs.

The formal business Accounting statement prepared to show financial position is the Balance Sheet, which lists the amounts of various assets of the business and the claims against these assets, or liabilities. A positive ratio on your Balance Sheet, though very desirable, is no indication or guarantee of a successful business, nor does a business have to be losing *money* to get into financial trouble.

Some new upstarts in business become prematurely over impressed with their company's assets. This can lead a business into trouble if the owner fails to recognize that business assets can and oftentimes do include receivables not yet collected, inventory not yet sold, borrowed funds, or loans at risk which may not be paid back, among other things.

Referring to our textbook definition, most Accounting calculations are performed to summarize transactions and to categorize *numbers*. Now, these categorizations may be of some interest to us at times, but the primary requirement of new business owners from the practice of Accounting is the comparison of income to costs and expenses. To accomplish this comparison, accountants generate what is known as an Income Statement, more popularly referred to as the Profit and Loss Statement or P&L.

Readers of this book are no doubt unanimous in their conviction that the primary objective of any business of any type is to earn a *profit*. It is paramount to keep in mind that a positive figure on the bottom line of your business P&L, even though it is preceded by a dollar sign, is a *number* and only a *number* termed *profit* that does not even exist in real time and has nothing to do with the measurement of *money* available to you.

Those business owners and entrepreneurs who are successful in the long run, acknowledge that *profit* is merely a *number* preceded by a dollar sign, which is mathematically calculated by subtracting all of the outstanding bills that you have in-hand but have not yet paid from income which has not necessarily been received.

Astute company operators realize this *number* known as *profit* or bottom line on the P&L statement is by no means any measure of *money* available for investing in the future of their enterprise. Too many men and women who start up their own viable business ventures fail to recognize the difference between *profit* and *money*.

This misconception can often lead a company down the road to ruin.

In the same manner, those business operators who fail to break the *five-year barrier* frequently confuse *money* with "cash-on-hand." This figure, listed on the firm's Balance Sheet as an asset is also a *number* which does not exist in real time. By the time a firm's Balance Sheet is compiled at the end of any month, quarter, etc., the actual amount of cash in the bank surely has changed. Of course, since the accrual Accounting method allows you to expense bills which have not yet been paid, the cash-on-hand balance is just another *number* which is not in itself a reference or measure of *money* available for future business purposes.

The only measurement in this context then of *money* accumulated and on hand for business development or expansion is the remainder of cash presently on hand at the bank, less all outstanding expenses or debt including long-term contracts and obligations. This measure..... Balance REmaining After Debt.....is easily summarized and humorously identified with the acronym BREAD.

Countless young business enterprises which exhibit a *profit* on their P&L statement have little or no BREAD. It is hereby recommended that you compute this measurement before undertaking capital expenditures of any kind. Indeed, it is not uncommon for a new business entity to complete its first year showing a *profit* and yet have to borrow *money* from the bank in order to pay income taxes on those same *profits*.

Numerous able and talented new business owners often mistake either cash-on-hand or *profit* for *money* and spend it. Despite abundant proficiency concerning a particular product, service or expertise, incorrect entrepreneurial business decisions regarding *money*, *numbers* and *profit* can permanently damage a company's financial position to the extent that a cash problem causes the business to close.

To demonstrate how a series of events could result in this situation, imagine this hypothetical scenario:

A talented well-respected Advertising Agency Executive through years of hard work and dedication to performance develops what is commonly referred to in the profession as a "hip-pocket" account billing two million dollars a year. Sensing these circumstances, the Account Executive advises his client of a long-held desire to start a new, small, but specialized ad agency. The client readily agrees to move the entire account to the new shop, lock, stock and barrel beginning January 1 of the following year.

Based on a standard fifteen percent commission, our Ad man can forecast solid agency revenue of three hundred thousand dollars for the first year (fifteen percent of two million). Since his client broadcasts and publishes a fairly even level of advertising on a year-round basis, he can also rely on a fairly even cash flow once the agency is up and running.

Further capitalizing on this opportunity, he convinces three of his co-workers at the Agency where he is employed to also leave their present employer and join him as partners in the new firm.

It must be stated here that even though some business ventures have been founded in the past along these lines, it is not advisable to start a new business these days in this fashion with the current complex legal environment surrounding anti-competitive employment agreements, the purloining of clients and/or employee piracy.

Estimating annual overhead expenses including office rent, furniture and equipment, postage, taxes, etc. at fifty thousand dollars as demonstrated in Illustration 1 on the following page, the four business partners figure they can afford a payroll of the remaining two hundred fifty thousand dollars and the new company will still break even at the end of its first year.

ILLUSTRATION 1

ADMAN ADVERTISING, INC.

Estimated Annual Overhead Expenses

At Breakeven

Office Rent	$ 12,000
Insurance	4,000
Legal	3,000
Accounting	3,000
Furniture & Equip. Rental	5,000
Stationery & Art Supplies	10,000
Telephone	3,000
Local Taxes & Licenses	3,000
Travel & Ent.	5,000
Utilities	1,000
Misc./Contingency	1,000
Total Overhead Expenses	$ 50,000
Projected Agency Income	$ 300,000
Available for Payroll	$ 250,000

Based on these calculations, they decide that each partner will receive a starting salary of fifty thousand dollars apiece and they will hire three clerical employees who will be paid an annual salary of fifteen thousand dollars each.

Under this plan, projected income compared with estimated costs and expenses for the first year is demonstrated in Illustration 2 below:

ILLUSTRATION 2
ADMAN ADVERTISING, INC.
Projected Income vs. Expenses

		MO	YR
Annual Income Projection			$ 300,000
Estimated Expenses		MO	YR
Salaries- Officers		$ 16,668	$ 200,000
Wages-Staff		3,750	45,000
Office Rent		1,000	12,000
Insurance		333	4,000
Legal		250	3,000
Accounting		250	3,000
Furn. & Equip. Rental		417	5,000
Stat. & Art Supplies		833	10,000
Telephone		250	3,000
Local Taxes & Licenses		250	3,000
Travel & Ent.		417	5,000
Utilities		83	1,000
Misc./Contingency		83	1,000
Total Monthly Expenses		$ 24,583	
Total Annual Expenses			$ 295,000

Armed with these data, the four partners are confident that the numbers accurately demonstrate the new agency is all but guaranteed to break even or better if they adhere to this operating budget of approximately twenty-five thousand dollars ($25,000) per month.

They then incorporate and issue themselves one thousand shares of common stock valued at $1 per share. On the first of January the business opens its doors and the four partners agree to borrow fifty thousand dollars from the local bank via a ninety-day note at nine and one-half percent annual interest, representing sufficient funds to cover operating expenses for the first two months. This is about the the period of time they foresee as necessary before the agency's cash flow will become positive.

Three months later on March 31, things are going just fine. These people are compatible, results-oriented professionals and the organization is operating without a hitch. The bank allows them to rollover the note for another ninety days upon payment of the interest due.

All continues to go well for this motivated group of new American entrepreneurs. When the company is six months old on June 30, the partners roll the note over again and the agency lands its second piece of business, an account billing an additional one million dollars. Now things are really starting to roll. The partners hire two twenty-five-thousand-dollar-a-year management employees, secure a little more office space and lease themselves company cars for business use. This increases salary and overhead expenses from twenty-five to thirty thousand dollars per month.

Before fiscal year-end the note is rolled over two more times. Once on September 30 and again on December 31. The first annual Income Statement (P&L) indicates a net profit after taxes of $30,000 on the bottom line, as shown in Illustration 3 on the following page.

Congratulations and celebrations abound. With an eye, but not necessarily his mind, on the American dream, our Adman and his partners decide to "plow" this thirty thousand dollar profit back into the

ILLUSTRATION 3

ADMAN ADVERTISING, INC.

Income Statement for Fiscal Year Ended

December 31, 19__

Agency Billing	$2,500,000	100%
Media & Production Costs	2,125,000	85%
Gross Revenue	$ 375,000	15%
Operating Expenses		
Interest	$ 4,250	
Office Rent	15,000	
Insurance	4,000	
Legal	3,000	
Accounting	3,000	
Furn. & Equip. Rental	5,000	
Stat. & Art Supplies	12,000	
Telephone	3,000	
Local Taxes & Licenses	3,000	
Travel & Ent.	5,000	
Utilities	1,000	
Auto Rent & Expense	6,000	
Salaries-Officers	200,000	
Wages-Staff	70,000	
Total Operating Exp.	$ 334,250	13%
Operating Profit	$ 40,750	2%
Fed. & St. Inc. Tax	$ 10,750	
Net Profit After Tax	$ 30,000	1%

business by purchasing, for cash, type-setting equipment they calculate will save the agency a good deal of money in the future. The equipment is installed and everything seems to be just fine as the young enterprise whirls into its second year of operation.

Three months later on the following March 31, the agency's current quarterly income statement (P&L) displays a year-to-date profit before taxes of over $20,000, as shown in Illustration 4.on the following page.

Despite the agency's profitability, however, when the bank calls the note due that same day, one year and three months after its inception, our newly established entrepreneurs find themselves in deep financial trouble, without the BREAD to pay the note. How did this happen? They failed to comprehend the difference between *money*, *numbers* and *profit*.

As mentioned, the agency opened its doors in January with fifty thousand dollars in borrowed funds and one thousand dollars from the sale of stock. Illustration 5 displays the agency's Cash Flow.

ILLUSTRATION 4

ADMAN ADVERTISING, INC.

Income Statement for First Quarter

Ended March 31, 19__

Second Year

Agency Billing	$ 750,000	100%
Media & Production Costs	637,500	85%
Gross Revenue	$ 112,500	15%
Operating Expenses		
Interest	$ 1,062	
Office Rent	3,500	
Insurance	1,000	
Legal	1,000	
Accounting	750	
Furn. & Equip. Rental	1,250	
Stat. & Art Supplies	2,500	
Telephone	750	
Local Taxes & Licenses	1,000	
Travel & Ent.	1,250	
Utilities	250	
Auto Rent & Expense	2,500	
Salaries-Officers	50,000	
Wages-Staff	25,000	
Total Operating Exp.	$ 91,812	12%
Operating Profit	$ 20,688	3%

ILLUSTRATION 5

ADMAN ADVERTISING, INC.

Cash Flow Statement

	January	February	March
Cash Balance	-	26,000	2,000
Loan Proceeds	50,000		
Cash rec'd/commissions	-	-	25,000
Cash from Common Stock	1,000		
EXPENSES			
Salaries-Officers	16,667	16,667	16,667
Wages-Staff	3,750	3,750	3,780
Rent	1,000	1,000	1,000
Art Supplies	833	833	833
Office Supplies	417	417	417
Travel & Entertainment	417	417	417
Auto Rent & Expense	-		
Interest	-		1,062
Insurance	333	333	333
Legal	500		500
Accounting	250	250	250
Telephone	250	250	250
Taxes & Licenses	500		
Utilities	83	83	83

ILLUSTRATION 5

ADMAN ADVERTISING, INC.

Cash Flow Statement

	April	May	June
Cash Balance	1,438	2,438	2,938
Loan Proceeds			
Cash rec'd/commission	25,000	25,000	25,000
Cash from Common Sto			
EXPENSES			
Salaries-Officers	16,667	16,667	16,667
Wages-Staff	3,750	3,750	3,750
Rent	1,000	1,000	1,000
Art Supplies	833	833	833
Office Supplies	417	417	417
Travel & Entertainmen	417	417	417
Auto Rent & Expense	-		
Interest	-		1,063
Insurance	333	333	333
Legal			
Accounting	250	250	250
Telephone	250	250	250
Taxes & Licenses		500	
Utilities	83	83	83

	July	August	September	October
	2,875	10,209	18,543	24,815
	37,500	37,500	37,500	37,500
	16,667	16,667	16,667	16,667
	7,916	7,916	7,916	7,916
	1,167	1,167	1,167	1,167
	833	833	833	833
	417	417	417	417
	417	417	417	417
	833	833	833	833
			1,062	
	333	333	333	333
	500		500	
	250	250	250	250
	250	250	250	250
	500		500	
	83	83	83	83

ILLUSTRATION 5

ADMAN ADVERTISING, INC.

Cash Flow Statement

	Novenber	December	January
Cash Balance	33,149	40,483	46,754
Loan Proceeds			
Cash rec'd/commission	37,500	37,500	37,500
Cash from Common Sto			
EXPENSES			
Salaries-Officers	16,667	16,667	16,667
Wages-Staff	7,916	7,916	3,750
Rent	1,167	1,167	1,167
Art Supplies	833	833	833
Office Supplies	417	417	417
Travel & Entertainmen	417	417	417
Auto Rent & Expense	833	833	833
Interest	-	1,063	
Insurance	333	333	333
Legal	500	500	500
Accounting	250	250	250
Telephone	250	250	250
Taxes & Licenses	500	500	500
Utilities	83	83	83
Income Taxes			
Equipment Purchase			30,000
Repayment of Loan Principal			

	February	March	April
	24,088	32,422	(22,056)
	37,500	37,500	
	16,667	16,667	
	7,916	7,916	
	1,167	1,167	
	833	833	
	417	417	
	417	417	
	833	833	
		1,062	
	333	333	
	250	500	
	250	250	
		250	
		500	
	83	83	
		10,750	
		50,000	

The business began generating cash on a steady, basis beginning in March as projected. Please note Cash from Commissions beginning in March. This number represents the amount of cash the business will receive during that month. Refer to the Beginning Cash Balance listed across the top of the chart immediately below each month. This number represents the amount of cash the business has available to spend at the beginning of that month after payment for expenses from the previous month.

As you can see by reading these numbers from left to right, this promising new advertising agency is forced to close its doors when the bank calls the note. If not for the decision to purchase type-setting equipment, funds would have been available to pay off the bank note and the firm would have continued to thrive.

Here is a concrete example of how a business can develop financial problems, even though it is showing a *profit* on the bottom line. In this case, you can readily see how our hypothetical new business owners put themselves into this precarious position by failing to realize *profit* is merely an arithmetically generated *number* preceded by a dollar sign, which is simply the remainder of income, including cash not yet received, less expenses and costs that have been incurred but not necessarily paid. The most significant point to remember here is that you can only spend *money*, you cannot spend *profit*. Once again, *profit* is not *money* in the bank available to you for spending or investing in the future of your company. It is only a *number* preceded by a dollar sign.

Money, *numbers* and *profit* are three different things. Those new business owners who succeed do not confuse them.

"As far as the laws of mathematics refer to reality, they are not certain; and as far as they are certain, they do not refer to reality."
-Albert Einstein

3

WORDS, INFORMATION AND LANGUAGE

CHAPTER THREE

WORDS, INFORMATION AND LANGUAGE

"Oaths are but words, and words but wind."
-Samuel Butler

Just as business is measured by *numbers*, it is most assuredly executed more often than not with *words*. The verb "execute"' however, can have positive (to carry on) or negative (to kill) connotations, and unfortunately, too many new entrepreneurs will fail within their first five years in business by confusing *words, information* and *language*.

A *word* is something that is said. *Language* is the method of combining words to communicate and *information* is the communication or reception of knowledge.

The majority of routine business transactions are being conducted verbally these days. With much deference to those futurists who foresee a video oriented society or "Global Village" heavily dependent once again on the spoken *word*, (even though reproduced), I offer another major reason contributing to this verbal business communication explosion in addition to the adaptation of modern technology. This phenomenon is being caused, in my opinion, by the increasing number of average American men and women from all walks of life entering the entrepreneurial ranks.

Since most of us probably feel we talk better than we write, a good number of individuals managing many of today's recently founded business operations prefer this manner of doing business on a day-to-day basis. It is often difficult for the average American to write well but we talk all the time. A poorly written business document or report may serve as lingering evidence of our literary shortcomings, while no one really expects our speech to be as well-constructed or polished as our writing.

Verbal communication has certain other advantages. The written word tends to etch our statements of position in stone, while in contrast, a speaker can adapt what he or she has to say depending on the listener's reactions. You can repeat what you have said when the listener is puzzled, speak faster if they show signs of being bored or even jump to another topic when the listener does not respond as you desire. You can obtain answers to questions and reactions to suggestions before you decide what to say next. You can even use facial expressions, voice tone or body language to add impact to your message.

On the other hand, when you are speaking, it is

easy to get off the subject or to ramble on. You do not always have the opportunity to catch your errors or to correct confusing statements. More importantly, you cannot always erase something you have already said.

Very few people, including ourselves, can remember exactly what was said or how we spoke. In addition, business agreements arrived at solely in a verbal manner can be very tricky and lead to unforeseen consequences.

In our own experience we are familiar with situations which occur daily when people communicating verbally misunderstand each other. One person or the other fails to interpret what was said in the way it was intended. How many times in your lifetime have you seen this happen, even among members of the same family? Or, as previously mentioned, memories differ regarding what was said. Oftentimes, there can be disagreement as to exactly what was agreed upon. Even if both parties to a conversation are forthright individuals who consider their *word* as their bond, miscommunication can still occur. The primary role of the written word in business therefore is to memorialize the spoken word in order to avoid this situation. There presumably was a time when all business transactions were handled verbally, but the introduction of the written word has allowed the conducting of commerce to advance (or decline) to the level of sophistication we find today.

Marshall McLuhan, the late media intellectual, put it more profoundly in his publication, *The Medium is the Message*: "The goose quill put an end to talk. It abolished mystery; it gave architecture and towns; it brought roads and armies, bureaucracy. It was the basic metaphor with which the cycle of civilization began, the step from the dark into the light of the mind. The hand that filled a parchment page built a city." [1]

Much in the same way as the Victorian era of the quill pen gave way to the typewriter in the early twentieth century, modern day technology provides those of us in business with a wide range of communication choices beyond simply writing it down or talking face-to-face. We can telephone, teletype, televise via closed circuit, use electronic taping, videotaping or employ some other method to get our message across.

The focus of this chapter however, is the written word. A significant number of professionals and entrepreneurs piloting a wide range of business operations, get these operations into trouble by failing to recognize how often the written word is utilized for purposes other than straightforward communication.

Even when the sole intention of business writing is the straightforward dispensing of information, that result is not always achieved. Alexander L. Sheff explains this dilemma in the popular Doubleday publication *How to Write Letters for all Occasions* as follows. "Many people think that there is a special language called 'Business English' which is supposed to be somewhat different from everyday spoken English. Frequently, this new concept complicates the job of writing to a person with whom you are doing business." 2

As we all know, a good number of business professionals and entrepreneurs, especially those involved in the technological arena, seem compelled not only to utilize buzzwords, technical terms and esoteric phrases, but to overuse them every chance they get.

Vast amounts of time, labor and *money* can be

wasted in this way. Robert L. Shurter, author of *Written Communications in Business*, a college-level textbook also designed as an instruction manual for those who are already engaged in business, asserts "Wordiness is without doubt the worst fault of all report writing style; it results in needless expense and waste. The investment that business, industrial, and research organizations put annually into reports is impossible to calculate, but it is unquestionably a huge sum." 3

Think about your own experience. How often have you been forced to suffer through a lengthy business instrument so chock full of jargon and mumbo jumbo, that it is rendered almost useless regarding what it is trying to communicate in the first place? Now consider this: if written business documents designed primarily to dispense information in a direct manner can be misinterpreted, imagine the potential for distaster brought about by business writing intentionally designed to do otherwise. It is under these circumstances that the importance of differentiating *words*, *information* and *language* becomes paramount to your success as a new business owner and to the survival of your operation.

There are two primary forms of business communication employing the written word which are not necessarily concerned with the absolute straightforward transmission of *information*. The first of these forms to be covered here is a component of the advertising industry known as *copy*; the second is a skill which lawyers refer to as writing *language*.

Advertising *copy* touches the lives of virtually all of us on a daily basis. We are literally bombarded with scores of messages to buy particular goods or services in our roles as both consumers and as new business owners. The craft of producing *copy* involves stringing words together to imply or to suggest ideas that are not necessarily being conveyed, in order to influence consumer buying behavior. *Copy* designed to communicate a benefit concerning a product or service dispenses only whatever *information* is necessary to substantiate this benefit, and no more. In a sense, the message stated via *copy* is not so much an outright lie, but more like a half truth, rather than the whole truth. In his revealing book, *I Can Sell You Anything*, which discloses dozens of the advertising industry's best-kept secrets regarding selling techniques, renegade Adman Carl P. Wrighter proclaims:

> Advertising...takes advantage of the license to dispense information, usually by giving us something less than pure fact. It's amazing, for instance, to discover how many "tests by independent laboratories" manage to rate different products in the same category, and

no two tests come out the same. Soap "A" finds an independent laboratory that proves conclusively their soap kills more bacteria than any other soap, while soap "B" uses an independent laboratory that proves conclusively their soap stops odor-causing germs better than any other soap. Maybe they're both facts, maybe not. Maybe they don't even have anything to do with each other, yet these two manufacturers can now go merrily about their business dispensing "information."

When we get ready to pitch a new soap at you, we know more about what you do in your bathroom than your own wife or husband. Not only that, we know why you do it, how you do it, and what makes you do it. We know what kind of appeals you respond to, what kind of emotions you will fall prey to, even the very words which will strike a chord on your heart strings. In short, persuasion in advertising is done not so much by dispensing information publically as by attacking your weak spots emotionally. 4

In his amusing and enjoyable work, *From Those Wonderful Folks Who Brought You Pearl Harbor*, Legendary Adman Jerry Della Femina, describes this same situation somewhat differently. "The quality of most advertising really depends on what has to be said. You're writing an ad on insurance, it's easy. It's great to do ads on the stock market. It's simple to do ads on a camera that gives you a picture sixty seconds after you shoot it. The big problem is the guy who has to do an ad for soap. Some poor son of a bitch is sitting in his office over at Compton right this minute trying to figure out what to say about Ivory Soap that hasn't been said maybe twenty thousand times before. I mean, what do you say? Where do you go? No matter what you say, it's still soap." [5]

Unfortunately, these knowledgeable authors are describing circumstances that are occurring in the advertising profession all too often these days. What amounts to literally billions of advertising dollars being spent in the United States alone each year has created a high-pressure environment to merchandise products and services which are not much different from one another, if not identical, on a scale so massive it is almost difficult to comprehend.

This intensely competitive climate has fostered the development of an occupation involving the ability to orchestrate the written word which is known as *copywriting*. Some of these skilled craftsmen earn enormous salaries by conceiving phrases which appear declarative to the untrained eye or ear, but are in fact somewhat spurious.

We are all familiar with claims contained in

commercials and advertisements for household products which promise to "work like" this, "act against" that or "help stop" the other thing. If a pharmaceutical company were to announce a new medication that "works like" a doctor's prescription to "help stop" hangover symptoms, for instance, no doubt this would simply be another pitch for plain old aspirin that has not been said maybe twenty thousand times before; possibly dreamed-up by the same poor son of a bitch Ivory Soap copywriter whom Della Femina envisioned working in his office over at Compton.

When a detergent manufacturer announces "Nothing Cleans Better" than a particular dish washing liquid, it probably means that the product cleans just as well as all the other brands in the same category, and nothing more. Fabricated expressions such as "home baked" (vs. homemade), "buttery flavor" (may or may not contain butter) and "lemon-fresh" (may or may not contain real lemons) serve to confuse what we think with what we hear. To our dismay, many of us are now discovering electronic gadgets which "never need batteries" do not necessarily last forever. They just run down eventually and are disposed of because the batteries cannot be replaced.

Other examples of combining words in a new way to say something old abound. This is not to say that all advertising is deceitful. A considerable amount of it is straightforward and truthful regarding the product or service it warrants, but the growing inventive and clever use of *copy* has made it increasingly difficult to separate the wheat from the chaff.

Regretfully this increase in the practice of clever *copy* has transcended consumer packaged goods broadcast marketing and is now becoming more and more prevalent in much business to business print advertising. Since entrepreneurs and professionals operating their own businesses are continuously buying products and services from vendors and suppliers, it is important that we learn to recognize and distinguish *copy* from *information*.

If a supplier's bulletin declares that your company has been "selected to receive" a special consideration, understand this may mean nothing more than being picked out of a hat at random rather than some unique honor.

Be wary of Insurance Companies who, while vying for your account, will publish rates lower than your present premium for "similar coverage." When it comes time to file a claim, you may find that the word "similar" does not necessarily mean "identical."

Your bank may assure you in writing that it offers the "highest interest rates in town." This indeed may be true but you can rest assured other local banks in your city are probably paying their customers the same interest rate as well.

If a client's purchasing agreement indicates an order "up to" a particular quantity of goods, do not immediately go out and buy materials or lease facilities sufficient to produce this quantity. The actual number of items ordered may wind up being much less than the maximum and you could be stuck with costly unsold inventory.

Watch out for purchase orders which promise you "payment within thirty days." You may expect remittance within thirty days of the shipping date or even thirty days from receipt of the merchandise at its required destination, but odds are you will receive payment thirty days from when the recipient gets your invoice in hand. If your billing process is not prompt and happens to be delayed for some reason, a serious cash flow problem might result.

I could go on and on relating additional specific examples of *copy*, but I will not. The key point to be acknowledged here is the significance new business owners must place on recognizing the difference between *information* and *copy*.

The area of business agreements and contracts in particular, brings us to the second form of business writing to be covered in this chapter---the slightly different but somewhat related talent for crafting the written word, which lawyers often refer to as writing *language*. The act of producing *language* is often described as drafting rather than writing, no doubt to reflect the refined skill or artistic capabilities required of the author.

In *The Official Lawyers Handbook*, Daniel Robert White, Esquire, begins his chapter titled Legal Writing as follows, "Everyone knows that legal writing is different than regular writing. People can understand regular writing." [6]

Mr. White, a fairly recent law school graduate, whose father, brother, aunt, uncle, great-uncle, and grandfather are or were all lawyers, displays an uncanny understanding of his understatement quoted above, demonstrated by what he outlines as the TEN PRINCIPLES OF LEGAL WRITING reproduced below.

PRINCIPLES OF LEGAL WRITING

1. Never use one word where ten will do.
2. Never use a small word where a big one will suffice.
3. Never use a simple statement when it appears that one of substantially greater complexity will achieve comparable goals.

4. Never use English where Latin, mutatis mutandis will do.

5. Qualify virtually everything.

6. Do not be embarrassed about repeating yourself.

   Do not be embarrassed about repeating yourself.

7. Worry about the difference between "which" and "that."

8. In pleadings and briefs, that which is defensible should be stated. That which is indefensible, but which you wish were true, should merely be suggested.

9. Never refer to your opponent's "arguments"; he only makes "assertions," and his assertions are always "bald."

10. If a layman can read a document from beginning to end without falling asleep, it needs work. 7

We are all able to recognize the tongue-in-cheek tone and appreciate the humor in what Mr. White writes, principally because of our personal experiences with lawyers and business contracts in the past. In spite of this, it is critical for those of us accountable for minding our own business to make certain the joke is not on us in the future.

Lawyers do seem to use big words rather than small ones, ten words where it appears one word will do and complex statements instead of simple straightforward sentences. This is the essence of drafting *language* for one reason and one reason only…..in order to produce business documents containing written statements which appear not unreasonable, but are in fact of major advantage to one party over the other.

In a more serious section of *The Official Lawyer's Handbook*, under the heading "The Myth of the

Reasonable Contract," attorney White reminds us, "Contracts, leases and the like, are not neutral documents. Lawyers draft them for specific clients and their terms invariably favor the client of the lawyer who drafted them. So one-sided are most documents, that lawyers' form files contain two versions of each type, one version drafted for one side, one for the other." [8]

If failing to recognize and identify *copy* can get a new business owner into trouble, the perils of misreading *language* are manifest since *language* appears in formal legal documents bearing our signatures which are designed by their very intent to be lawfully binding.

Now just as *copy* or *language* should not be accepted at face value, for *information*, this section should not be misread as an exercise in "lawyer bashing." Even though I do know of a famous outspoken Circuit Court Judge who served for thirty-five years in Cook County, Illinois and who on one occasion defined lawyers as "cats who settle differences between mice."

The point here is to impress upon you the absolute folly of wading into the world of minding your own business without the aid of an astute and competent professional lawyer. With nearly seven hundred thousand practicing attorneys in the United States alone, it should not be too difficult to find one knowledgeable in your field of endeavor.

Some of us know just enough legal terms and expressions to be dangerous when it comes to handling our own legal matters. We fancy ourselves a sort of Clarence Darrow or Perry Mason type. We throw legal terms around and when we're involved in certain business negotiations we talk too much. A good lawyer will not only assist us in getting out of sticky business situations, but more importantly, can help us prevent problems before they arise. Think about it. Hardly a day goes by in our legalistic and litigious society without some misunderstanding presenting itself as a possible legal trap.

Those of us charged with minding our own business are faced, for example, with all sorts of contracts. Some of them are simple enough but others can be quite deceptive.

New business owners can also get into trouble by considering contracts as guarantees of performance. Keep in mind, even if you do have an ironclad contract that promises delivery of a particular product or completion of a specific service by a certain date, this in no way guarantees that you will receive that product or service by that date. A contract can only provide recourse if the product is not delivered on time or if the service rendered is late and you suffer consequences accordingly. Of course, you must go to court, win your case, and then collect the judgment. By that time, your firm may have already suffered irreparable damage. If the legal fees don't bust you, your time and attention is taken from your business in its crucial early development stage. You will be spending all your time in your lawyer's office or in court.

Many struggling new business operations have been dragged down to failure by entanglement in needless legal complications. Here is a hypothetical example of how misinterpreting *language* caused severe harm to a relatively small privately-owned business.

In this case, a woman who owns a commercial art studio conceives the idea of securing the rights to well-known winter holiday paintings by popular

American artists, transforming them into miniature three-dimensional sculptures and reproducing them for sale as inexpensive Christmas tree ornaments.

Realizing permission from the artist must be obtained, she goes about contacting several appropriate painters and finally finds one agreeable to her offer. She is willing to pay the painter a royalty based on the number of ornaments sold. The painter, in turn, tells her he will require a minimum guaranteed payment up front.

The art studio owner then attends a meeting with the painter who is accompanied by his attorney and is presented with a licensing agreement which contains the following language buried among ten pages peppered with forthwiths, hereinafters and wherefores:

"Licensee agrees to pay to licensor a non-refundable advance payment of fifty-thousand dollars ($50,000) at the signing of this agreement representing a royalty of one cent ($.01) per item for the first five million items and also agrees to make an additional royalty payment of two cents ($.02) per item if the quantity sold exceeds five million items and three cents ($.03) per item if the quantity sold exceeds ten million items."

Our enterprising entrepreneur believes she understands the leverage being brought to bear by her collaborator. The more successful the product, the larger the share of the pie being demanded by the licensor. Since the item's success depends heavily on the popularity of the artist's paintings and the more ornaments sold, the more profit the art studio owner will make, she agrees to this condition rather than see her entire idea go up in smoke.

She subsequently proceeds to market and promote the item fully aware that regardless of the success or failure of the project she is out fifty thousand dollars, but also knows that she does not have to make any additional royalty payments to the painter unless she sells over five million ornaments. If this happens, she is confident that aggregate profits will more than cover this cost.

The program is a resounding success. Orders are received for over twelve million ornaments. The art studio owner is ecstatic as she sub-contracts a national manufacturer to produce this quantity based on her original sculptures.

Encouraged by this accomplishment, she is well underway developing another concept with a different licensor when a lawsuit filed by the painter's lawyer threatens the future of her business. What happened? There was a misinterpretation of *language*. At the conclusion of the program, the art studio owner promptly mailed a certified check to the painter in the amount of one hundred sixty thousand dollars based on the following calculations:

# Items	Royalties	Remarks	Balance
5,000,000	$.01	Prepaid	$0
5,000,000	.02	Per agree.	$100,000
2,000,000	.03	Per agree.	60,000
	TOTAL DUE:		$160,000

The painter's attorney immediately sent the check back with an invoice for three hundred sixty thousand dollars as follows:

Total # Items	Additional Royalties Due	Remarks	Balance Due
12,000,000	$.03	Per agree.	$360,000

Unfortunately for our art studio owner, a careful reading of the *language* incorporated in the license agreement plainly discloses that that an additional payment of $360,000 is due, representing an additional $.03 royalty for each of twelve million ornaments.

See how easily a new business owner can get into significant trouble by misinterpreting *language*! The two hundred thousand dollars in unexpected royalty payments can well represent most if not all of the *profits* anticipated by the art studio owner. Perhaps she had already invested some of these *profits* into her next venture. If so, her business problem is multiplied. In addition to misinterpreting *language*, she has also failed to differentiate between *money* and *profit*.

Circumstances such as these cause far too many entrepreneurs responsible for minding their own business to have serious problems and unnecessary difficulties when they misunderstand the written *word* by neglecting to correctly decipher between *information*, *copy* and *language*.

"Deeds are fruits. Words are leaves."
- *Bits & Pieces*

4

CHANCE, PROBABILITY AND RISK

CHAPTER FOUR

CHANCE, PROBABILITY AND RISK

"You pays your money and takes your choice."
-V.S. Lean

Starting a new business of your own is oftentimes a great *risk* with the genuine possibility of great financial loss. The majority of small business launches are funded and always have been by the personal savings of entrepreneurs. Many men and women, highly talented in their field or profession, suddenly find their business enterprise in dire straights because they fail to recognize the difference between *chance* and *probability*, with regard to the likelihood of severe monetary didaster within the first five years.

Everyone with the initiative to open his or her

own privately-owned company in America has a *chance* at success and fortune, and anybody can get lucky, but those individual business owners who are prosperous usually accomplish this feat by evaluating *risk* in a manner which clearly and unequivocally distinguishes between the *chance* that something might happen from its predictable but uncertain *probability* of occurrence.

Webster's New World Dictionary of the American Language describes *chance* as an accidental circumstance, *probability* as a *chance* stronger than possibility but falling short of certainty and *risk* as the *chance* or degree of *probability* of loss. An entrepreneur of course, is defined as a person who organizes and manages a business assuming the *risk* for the sake of *profit*.

Webster further explains *probability* as "a mathematical basis for prediction that for an exhaustive set of outcomes is the ratio of the outcomes that would produce a given event to the total number of possible outcomes." Fortunately, for those of us (including myself) who find this a rather difficult sentence to untangle, John E. Freund and Frank J. Williams, writing to instruct college Business Administration majors in their text titled, *Modern Business Statistics*, formally define *probability* as follows: "The proportion of the time an event takes place is called its relative frequency, and the relative frequency with which it takes place in the long run is called its *probability*."[1]

The focus of both these definitions is clear. The *probability* of a particular event occurring represents a fairly sophisticated mathematical calculation based on *information* specifying the number of times the event has already occurred over an extended period of time. In other words, assuming what happened in the past is an indication of what will occur in the future. We know, for example, that the probability of obtaining heads in the toss of a coin is .5 from experience in flipping a large number of such coins in the past.

If the probability in a particular retail service category of a business failing in the first five years is .7 if it opens independently and .3 if it is part of a national franchise chain, the smart move may indeed be to play the odds and become a franchisee. On the other hand, making the decision one way or the other according to these statistics would neither assure your success nor doom your business to failure. The above probability estimates indicate that in the long run all franchised retail businesses in this service category have been successful seventy percent of the time in the past, while independents have succeeded only thirty percent of the time. Of course, in this instance it appears fewer franchises will fail in the future than independent owners, but since we are talking about a specific event represented by a particular new business and you as an individual represent the most dominant variable affecting its success, you could win either way. If we calculate the probability of any flatbed shipment arriving on time is .85, does this mean the odds of our shipment not arriving on time is .15?

Peter Cohen, author of *The Gospel According to the Harvard Business School*, tells us, "The past (whether genuine or simulated) cannot tell you what will happen in the case of the one particular event you are trying to predict, because the flatbed you are looking at may just be the one out of a hundred that happens not to derail. But by giving you patterns and averages, the past can give you at least a feel for what might happen; it can tell you what the likely consequences will be. Which is a lot better than leaving things to *chance*."[2]

It is not meant to imply here that all business decisions can be neatly calculated arithmetically. Although many business decisions are based to a large extent on logic, which can sometimes be reduced to mathematical models, many more are not.

Unlike mathematics, business management is not an exact science. Therefore, no general mathematical formula exists to calculate the exact probability of any specific business endeavor's success. Individual business owners are not only confronted with the task of frequently developing our own formula, but we are often required to create a separate formula for each and every critical business situation we encounter.

Considering all facets of *information* when developing your particular formula to estimate the probability of success for any particular business venture is extremely essential. Far too many entrepreneurs put their new operations under by making faulty decisions in this area also based on the misuse or misunderstanding of *numbers*.

When *information* is available, previous personal experience must provide insight not necessarily indicated by numerical data. Creative and intuitive factors must address dimensions beyond the scope of the numbers if you expect yourself to succeed in the long run. You cannot let numbers make your decisions for you.

Numerical data, like the written *word*, should never be accepted at face value as *information*. Remember, *numbers* are not always what they seem and erroneous confidence concerning the nature of *numbers* can lead to gross discrepancies when estimating probabilities. More importantly, mathematical calculations alone should never be mistaken for comprehensive analysis.

This is not to say that mathematical calculations should not be used whenever possible in deciding your direction, or that numerically computed solutions are always wrong. But allowing numbers or their manipulation to govern rather than influence your decisions can cause grave consequences for your business.

In many cases you may feel unable to determine from past information or prior experience a suitable estimate of probability. Under such circumstances, however, you must make an estimate of the *risk* entailed on the basis of your general knowledge of the problem under consideration.

This task can largely be accomplished by reviewing the past history of similar events to determine any *information* helpful in spotting trends to evaluate the current situation and then using these data to predict the likelihood of the event occurring again in the future. This is, no doubt, an imperfect form of analysis, but nonetheless, far better than no analysis at all.

The successful business owner or entrepreneur does not fear *risk*. In fact, taking calculated *risks* is one of the things that minding your own business is all about. Calculated beyond numerical data via a formula which also includes creative and relative intuitive factors when estimating the *probability* of a future event.

On the other hand, we must recognize that in determining the probability of a particular event occurring, situations may arise where false intuition can be disastrous.

To demonstrate how many new business owners get their companies into trouble through incorrect assumptions in this area, let's use our imagination and personify three entrepreneurial types whom we will call the "Anticipant Gambler," the "Big Picture Opportunist," and the "Hard-Nosed Mathematician."

Say we find ourselves in a casino standing by a booth containing a large, numbered wheel. People are placing bets on various numbers before each spin of the wheel and if their number comes up, they win. If not, they lose. For the sake of simplicity, let us assume there are ten sections on the wheel, numbered one through ten consecutively.

Up walks our "Anticipant Gambler" who happens to consider seven as his lucky number. As we observe, he promptly bets on the number seven accordingly. The wheel spins and stops at five. He places another bet on seven. The wheel comes up eight. Again he bets *money* on the number seven but this time the winning number is nine. We watch this procedure go on for some time. He continues betting on the number seven and he keeps losing *money*. His bets become larger and larger as he attempts to recoup his loses but this just causes him to lose more *money* at a faster rate. This ritual may last until his funds are completely exhausted.

You see, every time the "Anticipant Gambler" plays and loses, he figures that the *probability* of the wheel stopping at number seven increases because it is *due*. When in actuality, the odds of winning on any one number are one in ten with each spin of the wheel – no more, no less – no matter how long he stays there watching the wheel. In other words, he will lose ninety percent of the time over the long run. In much the same manner, "Anticipant Gamblers" in business for themselves wind up as losers more often than not.

Let us leave this "Anticipant Gambler" to his own devices and examine the example of the "Big Picture Opportunist" by moving from the wheel to a table where a heads or tails coin toss game is being played. The rules of the game are simple. The first flip of the coin is free but before you can toss the coin again, the house requires you to place a bet and agrees to pay double your money if the coin comes up tails.

We see a "Big Picture Opportunist" stroll over to the table. He flips the coin the first time and it comes up heads. The house then offers to pay him double any wager he cares to make if his second toss comes up tails. He concludes that in the long run the law of averages stipulates half the time the coin will land tails up. Therefore, since he has already flipped heads, he reasons to himself that according to the big picture the probability is now better that he will get a tail. Based on this erroneous assumption, he bets all he has in order to take full advantage of what he considers to be an excellent opportunity. Unfortunately, the coin comes up heads and he loses everything.

What he failed to recognize is that the second flip is not influenced by the first in any way whatsoever. The odds of getting heads or tails remain the same with each flip of the coin. "Big Picture Opportunists" running their own businesses usually fall prey to false opportunities envisioned by misunderstanding the laws of *probability*. They then compound their problems by taking *risks* greater than necessary in hopes of cashing in on the Big Deal.

After viewing the demise of the "Big Picture Opportunist," suppose we now linger at the coin toss table long enough to witness the outcome when a "Hard-nosed Mathematician" steps up to play the game. His first flip of the coin comes up tails. The house then offers him the same wager, to double his money if his second toss also comes up tails. Secure in the knowledge that when we flip a coin we can get one or the other, but not both, he realizes the *probability* of the coin coming up either heads or tails is one-half. The "Hard-nosed Mathematician" then correctly calculates that the *probability* of getting tails in two successive flips of a coin is one in four. Deciding he does not like the odds he refuses to bet any amount and walks away from a fifty-fifty proposition, which in terms of mathematical expectations is considered by professional statisticians to be a very fair and equitable game.

Even though the *probability* of getting tails in two successive flips of a coin are indeed one in four, this fact has nothing to do with the circumstances in which our "Hard-Nosed Mathematician" finds himself. He had already flipped tails. Once again, the odds of tails then coming up on the second toss are not affected whatsoever by the first toss and also remain fifty-fifty.

Digging for data and manipulating numbers and subsequently using them incorrectly can lead to many poor and sometimes fatal business decisions. "Hard-Nosed Mathematicians" can miss numerous sound business opportunities. They tend to seek answers to everything in arithmetic and often substitute computation for deliberation.

As we leave our imaginary casino you may feel as if you are already familiar with one or more, or even all of these characters. The "Big Picture

Opportunist" like the "Anticipant Gambler" is guilty of false intuition concerning the rules of *probability*. The "Hard-Nosed Mathematician" is responsible for letting numerical calculations get in the way of properly calculating *risk* to determine the *probability* of success.

Take the hypothetical case of two recent Med School Graduates who were classmates at the same Medical College and completed their internship at the same General Hospital. Both physicians go into private business practicing family medicine. Five years later, one is still struggling, while the other has a successful practice that has been growing steadily and will continue to grow and become more prosperous in the future. How did this happen?

Each doctor set out in his own manner to decide the location of his new practice. Doctor A, being the practical type, determined in his own mind that if he opened his practice in a section of the country where the number of doctors per capita was low, he would have a good chance at success. Off he went to a small town in the Midwest.

Doctor B, possessing a more methodical nature, thoroughly studied all the statistics he could obtain concerning the medical health-care industry. He studied population statistics and lifestyle trends. His careful analysis of demography indicated that the percentage of the population fifty years of age or older was growing and would continue to grow.

His review of economic and lifestyle data illustrate a geographic shift in the population as well. A great number of people were relocating to the Sunbelt, especially that segment of the population now reaching retirement age. He reasoned that if he opened his practice in a Sunbelt retirement city, he could capitalize on these two emerging factors. As people get older they require more health care and his practice would be located in an area of the country to which these older citizens were migrating. Off he went to the Gulf Coast of Florida.

Can you guess which doctor is successful and which one is still struggling? If you think Doctor B is our success story you are absolutely wrong.

You see, Doctor B fell into the trap of letting *numbers* make his decision for him and failed to consider dimensions beyond the numerical data, the most important of which in this case turned out to be his own age.

Senior citizens residing in the Sunbelt retirement communities had difficulty patronizing a relatively young doctor. They pre-judged his youth as inexperience and were unable to relate their medical concerns to a man so much younger. They felt self-conscious. Therefore, Doctor B's practice suffered from the start.

Doctor A's experience was entirely the opposite. The residents of the small Midwestern town were delighted to have a new doctor available since physicians were so scarce in that part of the country. People there even regarded his youth as somewhat of a novelty. Patients of all ages came from near and far to be treated for common illnesses, injuries and a wide variety of other ailments. Consequently his practice started to thrive from day one.

Successful individuals in business for themselves must look beyond statistics and not rely solely on numerical data to plot the future course of their enterprise. Moreover, business owners who take *chances* without properly assessing the *probability* of success sadly contribute to the astonishing statistics regarding the extremely high percentage of business failures within the first five years. Successful entrepreneurs who do shatter the *five year barrier* are *those who* appreciate the value of distinguishing *probability* from *chance* when evaluating *risk*.

The principal aspect of this quality is captured superbly by Anthony Jay, the British author of *Management and Machiavelli*, in his chapter titled "Risk and Restraint."

Wellington, Nelson, Marlborough, Montgomery, despite the glamorous, dashing aura which surrounds their names, always tried to make sure that they were not risking more than they could afford to lose, and were prepared to break off whenever a calculated risk appeared to be moving beyond their calculations. The hallmark of the great Generals has been their extreme skill in working out the risk. They really seemed to have anticipated S.J. Simon's advice to bridge players,* namely to work out before any bid or play the answers to three questions:

> How much can this win?
>
> How much can it lose?
>
> What are its chances of success? [3]

*S.J. Simon, *Why You Lose at Bridge* (London: Nicholson & Watson, 1945) P. 11.

"It may be that the race is not always to the swift, nor the battle to the strong – but that's the way to bet."

- **Damion Runyon**

5

ACTIVITY, PRODUCTIVITY AND PLANNING

CHAPTER FIVE

ACTIVITY, PRODUCTIVITY AND
PLANNING

"In all things, success depends upon previous preparation, and without such preparation, there is sure to be failure."
-Confucius

Men and women who are successful at minding their own business realize that possessing a strong desire to succeed by itself is simply not enough. This desire must be accompanied with the will to prepare.

Most entrepreneurs and new business owners have no trouble whatsoever keeping busy, but many get their companies into trouble by neglecting to distinguish between *activity* (being busy) and *productivity* (getting something accomplished).

Within some large corporations today, to borrow from a familiar quotation, it seems the business of American business is being busy. The large corporate environment often allows individuals to advance up the management ladder by displaying a high level of *activity* and simply promoting this characteristic to their superiors. Looking busy rather than being *productive* becomes their goal.

In fact, it is possible that some executives of major corporations have been promoted at every level in advance of completing many initiated projects. Frequently, as executives climb higher and higher up the corporate management ladder, they find themselves spending more and more time involved in organizational politics instead of utilizing their talents or professional skills to benefit the corporation. A large number of upwardly mobile corporate executives eventually wind up putting in long hard hours disciplining subordinates, impressing upper management and avoiding being eased out of power as they grow older. Their days are spent generating memoranda, talking on the telephone, attending meetings or traveling between one and the other *activity* with the sole objective of advancing to the next rung of the ever-narrowing corporate ladder ahead of their peers.

There are even special reports and seminars for sale to corporate executives by Management Consulting Companies with titles such as *How to Win at Organizational Politics*, promising to help corporate executives emerge as winners by providing them with instruction regarding common political challenges of tricky or unethical colleagues within the corporation. These "management education" courses address topics such as *Are Others Stealing the Credit You Deserve? Is a Subordinate After Your Job? How to*

Protect Yourself from Corporate Hatchet Men, How to Keep Pushy Employees from Presuming on Your Friendship, How to Get Out from Under the Shadow of a Domineering Boss, Might You be Scuttled by Disgruntled Subordinates? When a Two-Faced Employee Bad Mouths You Behind Your Back and *Are Employees Going Over Your Head in Secret?*

This is a perfect example of *activity* versus *productivity*.

For those of us who choose for whatever reason not to be corporate executives but to operate our own business, there is no advancement through mere *activity*. The only *activity* worthwhile if you are minding your own business is planned *activity* which produces results, or *productivity*. Now that you're an entrepreneur, your role has indeed changed and your success involves an emphasis on *planning* and less on doing.

Planning your business is your most important job now that you have opened your own operation. The principal management function of the small business owner is to anticipate the future and to *plan* a program of *action* determining what it is you want to accomplish and how you want to accomplish it.

One of the basic principles of minding your own business is to spend time making your enterprise a success by concentrating on the skills you have developed through practicing your trade or profession. Those skills which have enabled you to strike out on your own!

But many entrepreneurs starting out get too involved in running their business on a day-to-day basis by performing routine tasks and duties themselves which should be delegated to employees. This diminishes the proportion of their time which they can spend *planning*. More often than not, these small business operators work hard hours, sacrificing social interests and family life for the cause of the enterprise only to see their business fail like so many others. Those new business owners who allow themselves to be consumed by *activity* often feel they cannot afford to waste time *planning*. They fail to realize the best way to save time is to spend it wisely. By failing to *plan* they are *planning* to fail. New business owners who succeed in the long-run are those who take the time to concentrate on their company's future, not just its immediate situation.

Other prime examples of confusing *activity* with *productivity* abound. Some new business owners have the unproductive tendency to spend too much time and energy worrying about how best to invest the company's assets or how to save *money* by finding ways not to pay taxes.

One of the greatest mistakes made by new business owners who fail within the first five years is belief in the misconception that since the Government allows interest payments made on a business loan to be deducted from your company's taxable income, it is somehow to your advantage to borrow *money*.

Successful entrepreneurs realize that just because you can reduce taxes by borrowing *money*, there is absolutely no reason to borrow *money* if you don't have to.

You see, even though the interest cost is tax deductible, all this really means is that your tax bill will be reduced by a fraction of the amount of interest you paid. And you still must generate the extra cash to pay the entire interest and principal amount of the loan.

For example, let's say that a business owner

operating an enterprise with *profit* before taxes of $50,000 borrows $10,000 for one year and is charged an annual rate of ten percent. Therefore, he is then able to deduct a total of $1,000 from his company's taxable income. At a corporate tax rate of 30%, his taxes have been reduced by $300. However, after making the interest payment of $1,000 to the bank, he or she is still $700 poorer than if he had not borrowed the *money* in the first place, not to mention the cash flow ramifications which may be involved in paying the lender the full amount of the $10,000 in a timely manner, as demonstrated in the case involving Adman Advertising, Inc. outlined in Chapter two.

Yet the above example illustrates only one disadvantage of borrowing *money* to save taxes. Have you ever wondered why Uncle Sam would want to encourage you to borrow *money*? It's simple. The Government wants you to spend it.

Not only does this create income to others which will also be taxed, but eventually you must repay the loan principal to the lender.

Assuming our hypothetical business owner has spent the *money*, where will the $10,000 come from when it is time to pay up? That's right, you guessed it, from his BREAD. And at a 30% tax rate, in order for him to have $10,000 extra cash on hand after taxes, his company must generate approximately $15,000 in additional *profit* and pay almost $5,000 more to the Government in taxes.

You can see by this example how borrowing $10,000 needlessly and then spending it can cost a business about $5,700 in return for saving $300 in taxes.

It simply doesn't make sense for most small companies to borrow *money* needlessly in order to save taxes. Pay your fair share of taxes and concentrate on future business activities. As Benjamin Franklin stated, "In this world nothing can be said to be certain, except for death and taxes." Humorist J.L. Rogers had this to say on the same subject, "There is little to admire in bureaucracy, but you've got to hand it to the Internal Revenue Service."

The *planning* process conducted by the small business owner does not have to be fancy or complicated. You don't need a *planning* committee to set goals and objectives.

Frank F. Gilmore's comprehensive article titled "Formulating Strategy in Smaller Companies" included in the *Harvard Business Review on Management* offers this advice, "Judgement, experience, intuition and focused well-guided discussions are the key to success, not staff work and mathematical models. [1]

However, we do need to be able in some manner to predict future events in order to develop appropriate plans.

Although reliance on predictive approaches may sometimes be highly useful, caution must be exorcised in their application. This caveat is because many models are essentially "static," based on the not necessarily valid premise that the relationships between variables will be the same in the future as they've been in the past. If we could be certain of a particular future event occurring, we could simply calculate the return or payoff expected from each alternative strategy and then select whatever strategy provided the highest returns in term of our objectives. In most cases, however, we cannot determine exactly what events will occur and sometimes feel as if we can make no estimate whatsoever.

As disused in the previous chapter, under these

circumstances we must evaluate the *risk* entailed in our decision making on the basis of general knowledge of the problem under consideration.

Some of the time, we all find it necessary to settle for predictive data less accurate than we would like to have because of the excessive expense which would be incurred in obtaining highly precise information, or most often, because not enough time is available to develop such data.

The effectiveness of your *planning* efforts will usually be a function of the actions undertaken by your business itself, but the gathering and analysis of relevant data, statistical or otherwise, should not be mistaken for the task at hand and should be recognized for what it is – *activity*. Your *planning* efforts must lead to action in order to be *productive*.

Of course, we want to compile and review as much pertinent information as possible in the *planning* process, but there is such a thing as overplanning. The best plan possibly conceived is worthless if it is not implemented in a timely fashion.

Successful entrepreneurs are always careful to avoid what veteran business journalist Ray Rowan, author of *The Intuitive Manager*, terms "analysis paralysis," a condition caused by too much inquiry. In Rowan's opinion, constantly accumulating new information, without giving the mind a chance to percolate and come to a conclusion intuitively is substituting study for courage and can delay any important decision until the time for action has passed.2

An inability to decide on a course of action and putting off decisions by constantly needing more information can only lead to your downfall.

Andrew Jackson, seventh President of the United States, put it this way over a century ago, "Take time to deliberate: but when the time for action arrives, stop thinking and go in."

As Theodore Roosevelt, twenty-sixth President of the United States, said back in 1917, ""Nine-tenths of wisdom is being wise on time."

Let us examine the following hypothetical example concerning two partners who open a small hair salon in a strip shopping center. Both are highly talented stylists and each attracts a core clientele of faithful customers when they leave their respective employers and open their own shop. The business is humming right along shortly after they open their doors. Within three months the daily appointment calendars are filled and they find themselves turning away customers. They decide to open six days a week instead of five but soon thereafter once again find themselves with more customers than they can handle. The business is booming. Since both work full time attending to customers, opening and closing the shop as well as attending to the standard necessary business administrative and financial duties each day, they have very few hours left in their already busy schedules. They find themselves working harder and longer than they ever have before. Twelve hours a day, six days a week, with little time left for themselves or to spend with family and friends.

Before long, to their surprise, another hair salon opens on the far side of the same shopping center (no doubt due to the clever use of *language* in the landlord's lease). Initially, this new competitor has absolutely no impact since there is plenty of business to go around. As time goes by, however, business begins to slacken. Over time, it continues to slacken until eventually the enterprise is in serious trouble. What circumstances caused this turn of events?

While our partners were busy cutting and styling hair, their competitor was developing and implementing a plan of action designed to achieve success. The new competitor offered special promotional discounts, expanded their capacity when business demand warranted and provided supplementary services such as facials, manicures and pedicures. They even added a tanning bed and featured complete cosmetic makeovers. As a result of this astute business *planning* and timely implementation, the competitor wound up with most of the available customers and our previously successful partners were faced with becoming another statistic.

In the previous chapter I used the game of bridge to illustrate an approach in differentiating *chance* from *probability*. Fred Reinfeld, author of *How to Be a Winner at Chess* has this advice for those who follow his twelve basic rules for winning play. "Above all, following these rules helps you to be a winner at chess because they give you an objective; they give you a method for starting the game. This spots you a definite advantage over the vast majority of players who start the game in a mood of aimless drifting. Aimlessness is a likely prelude to losing. Purposeful play is an aid to setting up winning positions." 3

In business as in chess, *planning* ahead and recognizing the difference between *activity* and *productivity* is extremely crucial.

Of course, we cannot see into the future with any certainty, but it is essential to our success that we try. Besides, forecasting the future can oftentimes help us to create it.

In addition, it may be impossible to predict the *probability* of future calamities that are out of our control like economic downturns or shifting consumer attitudes, yet by considering their possibilities, *planning* often enables us to identify *risks* that might otherwise not have been recognized until it is too late.

A number of different values may be obtained by your organization from effective *planning* efforts. Underlying all these, however, is one basic function which *planning* your *activity* serves to perform – to help you increase the *probability* of occurrence of future *activity* which must take place if your objectives are to be attained. Taking the time to *plan* in itself is no assurance of success, but implementing a *plan* of action in a timely fashion is the only way to transform *activity* into *productivity*.

"Your future depends on many things, but mostly on you."
- *Frank Tyger*

6

EMPLOYEES, PERSONNEL AND PEOPLE

CHAPTER SIX

EMPLOYEES, PERSONNEL AND
PEOPLE

"Never tell people how to do things. Tell them what to do and they will surprise you with their ingenuity."
-General George S. Patton, Jr.

One of the greatest motivators of all time, old "Blood and Guts" summarized what is probably the most important element of successful employee relations when he uttered the above phrase.

One of the most powerful factors influencing how *people* feel about themselves is their job. Pay, benefits and working conditions are all important to *employee* morale, but even more so is an individual's feeling of self-achievement.

The greater the contribution that *people* have an opportunity to make, the more satisfaction and sense of accomplishment they will experience from their work.

In the previous chapter I used the game of chess to illustrate an approach in differentiating *activity* from *productivity*. In the game of chess, the players are just as important as the plays. And so it is in business. *People* are your most valuable asset and your ability to lead others effectively will contribute immensely to the *productivity* of your operation.

Now that you have started your own business, you have crossed an important line. No longer does your future depend only on what you can accomplish yourself, as much as it will depend on how much you can accomplish through the *people* who work for you.

New business owners who break the *five year barrier* recognize that they now must rely on the skills of other *people* and that the success of their enterprise rests largely on the willingness of their *employees* to get the job done. Entrepreneurs who overlook this principle often commit the error of focusing on low pay in an attempt to squeeze as much as possible from their *employees*, who usually respond by doing only the minimum amount of work required to keep their jobs. Of course it is necessary to keep an eye on costs and expenses, but no business, large or small, ever saved itself into prosperity. Do not confuse business efficiency with *productivity* when deciding what to pay your *people*.

One of the principal components of any small business success is captured by the often heard play-on-words that you can tell a company by the *people* that it keeps. As the founder, you may well be the head of your company, but reliable, trustworthy and dedicated *employees* are the backbone of any successful business enterprise.

A large number of business owners, however, find themselves at odds with their *employees* as opposed to being united in a common cause. When this occurs, *productivity* often gives way to mere *activity* as you are forced to spend an inordinate amount of your time dealing with what are commonly referred to as *personnel* problems.

Much has been said and written in recent years regarding *employee* motivation. And many attempts have been advocated by management science experts and tried by companies of all sizes and shapes to motivate *employees* with outside forces like incentives and rewards for job performance which should already be expected, only to be disappointed by the results.

More and more management scientists are coming to the conclusion that an individual's motivation, be it on the job or anywhere, comes from within.

Most *people* already have inner drives (motives) to do well. They are usually willing to become part of a team with common goals and a shared vision of what needs to be done, provided they are treated with respect and dignity as individuals. *People* generally crave greater recognition, and a chance to feel that what they do really matters. But a person who is not interested in obtaining more responsibility cannot be motivated into doing so.

George S. Odiorne, author of *The Human Side of Management* separates *employees* into four categories and offers the following advice:

"The first category includes the workhorses.....those who do a good job but won't blaze many trails. The second category includes the stars. These people do a superior job and have lots of potential for advancement. The third category are the problem children....those with lots of potential who are not fulfilling it in their present jobs. And the fourth category includes the deadwood. These people have low potential and aren't even performing adequately in their present job.

"Let your workhorses know what is expected of them and where they can go for help. Then give them freedom. Don't breathe down their necks if their track record is good. If we've learned anything at all from the behavioral sciences, it is that when people are encouraged to monitor their own work, this self-control releases their best energies.

"Managing the stars relies pretty much on the same principles, with this exception: stars will be trained, managed and often mentored with the specific aim of developing their potential and preparing them for higher responsibilities.

"Managing the problem children should be remedial....aimed at personal or situational factors that prevent them from fulfilling their high potential.

"As for the deadwood, for whom no existing or foreseeable remedies show any promise of improvement, further time and effort spent on development will be fruitless and wasteful."[1]

To effectively inspire those individuals who are self-motivated, however, you must delegate responsibility, authority and accountability in order to help them reach their full potential. Making someone responsible for their own work is only the first step in an *employee's* development. You must also grant authority by allowing them to do whatever is necessary to get the job done in their own way and then fix accountability by checking to see how they are doing from time to time.

There is a vast body of knowledge available concerning organizational behavior, group dynamics and *employee* motivation. Most is generated by behavioral scientists for study by other behavioral scientists, but there is one general rule regarding human relations which you should keep in mind at all times, especially now that you are responsible for minding your own business. We can work effectively with *people* only if we are prepared to think about them in human terms, as individuals who have deeply held values, varied backgrounds and different points of view.

Although a small company's *employees* may share a common workplace, each person is also individually different in a number of ways from physical makeup and physiological profile to fingerprints, for example. It therefore seems obvious that the most effective way to manage *employees* with individual differences is by treating them differently. Many small business operators overlook this evident fact and fail to follow this simple rule. They treat their *employees* like *personnel* instead of *people* and wonder why they are plagued with inefficient operations, uncooperative workers and high turnover. Broad rules and general orders are the nemeses of the small business organization.

There is simply no excuse for the small business owner who gets into trouble due to *employee* relations. The negative dynamics of organizational behavior which tend to manifest themselves in large corporations can usually be attributed to unavoidable breakdowns in communication, coordination and involvement.

Keith Davis, Ph.D. and author of *Human Relations At Work – The Dynamics of Organizational Behavior* calls this the "behemoth syndrome" which he describes as follows, "...increasing size develops a series of interrelated symptoms and problems. For example, large size is associated with lower employee satisfaction, which tends to increased absenteeism. Absenteeism, in turn, complicates coordination because most jobs are highly interdependent. Less coordination increases job frustration and probably reduces morale and productivity. Less coordination and reduced productivity, in turn, lead to new work pressures, rules, and problems, thereby making the system self-regenerating in its effect on human relations."[2]

As the leader of a small organization, you are fortunate to not have to deal with syndromes of this type caused by sheer size. Unlike large corporate organizations, when operating a small business, a much greater percentage of information exchanged with *employees* can be conducted via face-to-face conversation. You are often able to communicate one-on-one with the *people* who work for you.

This close-knit, verbal contact provides the perfect environment for clear two-way communication by allowing immediate reaction to feedback and instant response concerning questions or points of clarification as discussed in Chapter three.

Communicating person-to-person is probably the biggest single advantage small companies have over large corporations. By their very nature, large corporations cannot treat each individual differently but the small business operator can be mindful of individual differences.

It is important to note, however, that your role as a business owner should not require you to adopt another personality. You must distinguish between treating *people* differently and trying to be a different person to different *people*. The latter is not only a poor business practice, but could also lead to schizophrenia.

All too often, however, small business owners who are indeed cognizant that *employees* are different from one another, still cause their own "personnel problems" by failing to realize that they themselves are different also. In their attempts at *personnel* motivation, they make the mistake of automatically assuming that their *employees'* point-of-view is identical to their own and thereby forfeit the fundamental benefit of one-on-one human interaction.

The ancient Greek philosopher Socrates, who believed in the superiority of speaking over writing, taught Plato that the principle method of intellectual investigation is discussion and reasoning by dialogue.

In these modern times, *The Book of Business Knowledge* offers the following advice:

- You and your subordinates will almost *never* (italics original) see a problem the same way. Your experiences and perspectives are different. Stop before you delegate or discipline. Find out by good interviewing how the other person perceives an issue before you do anything about it.

- Before you get progress or agreement on an issue involving another person, there must be agreement that there is a problem. Then it is relatively easy to agree on a solution that meets conflicting needs.

- Feedback on performance and positive encouragement are the sources of improved motivation. Ignorance of results and/or a climate of criticism are the two most common sources of apathy and lack of motivation.[3]

Here is a hypothetical example of how treating *people* as individuals improved *employee* performance, halted the failure and contributed to the success of one small company.

An enterprising research manager leaves his corporate employer, goes out on his own and opens a telemarketing company designed to conduct weekday evening marketing surveys for product manufacturers and advertising agencies.

The firm will conduct interviews from 6 PM to 10 PM, Monday through Friday. Since each survey is designed to take approximately 3 minutes, our new business owner estimates that a phone tech should be able to complete 15 questionnaires per hour with a minute to spare between each interview.

He determines the firm needs to employ a minimum of 10 phone techs in order to meet customer sample requirements on a timely basis. He rents sufficient space, makes the hires, sets his prices so they're competitive and is fortunate to open with enough contract work to keep his staff busy.

Each phone tech is presented with a computer printout when they arrive for work, listing the names and telephone numbers of 60 different people and are expected to interview the complete list each evening.

To his dismay, our research manager discovers that some phone techs regularly fail to complete their nightly quota of surveys while others would always finish early and sit idle at their work station until quitting time – sometimes for as long as 30 minutes.

When he reprimands the more proficient interviewers for sitting idle and not helping other phone techs, he finds this approach simply causes them to work slower. Morale sinks, *productivity* suffers and a survey backlog develops. Customer deadlines are threatened to such a dangerous degree that he is impelled to take a new approach with his *employees* who finish their work ahead of the others.

He informs the phone techs, on a one-to-one basis, that when they complete their nightly quota they are free to get coffee or soft drinks and visit any other work station.

When the fast workers start visiting each other's work station every night, the slower phone techs soon start working faster because they too want time to socialize like the others.

At the same time, friendships develop as the faster workers visit other work stations and a considerable amount of informal training and help for the slower workers takes place.

Before too long, schedules are back in order and our research manager's commendable enterprise is back on track and rolling.

In this example, the owner first assumed that all *employees* understood the importance of efficiency in the operation and would freely contribute to its success. This assumption ignores the concept of "individual differences" between business owners and *employees*. Recognizing and treating each *employees* as an individual with respect and dignity proved to be the successful way of motivating them in this case.

In a small organization, fellow workers can and often do become part of each other's support group, providing encouragement and reinforcement for each other.

As mentioned in chapter one, over half-a-million new small businesses are opened each year. The people who open these businesses are usually former *employees* of competing companies who see better ways of doing things.

If you think of your *employees* as *people*, like you, and encourage them to channel their drive for improvement to perform their functions better, they can contribute fully to the overall success of your business. Treating *employees* like *personnel*, on the other hand, invites them to initiate these improvements elsewhere.

Many small business owners get entangled in *"personnel* problems" because they fail to realize first of all that each *employee* is a separate, distinct individual and secondly, that the plural form of person is *people* not *personnel*.

"People who need people are the luckiest people in the world."

-   **Barbara Streisand**

7

CONSUMERS, CUSTOMERS AND CLIENTS

CHAPTER SEVEN

CONSUMERS, CUSTOMERS AND CLIENTS

"Everyone lives by selling something."
- *Robert Lewis Stevenson*

Big corporations dependent on mass-marketing today are confronted with the challenge of improving the sale of their products to a faceless, elusive composite known as the American *consumer*. To do this they divide the population into what are called, "market segments."

These giants of industry spend large sums of money for research studies classifying people into groups, in order to identify and find what modern marketers describe as a product's *TARGET AUDIENCE.*

Numerous surveys have been conducted over the years by government, business and behavioral scientists to categorize or group people together in many ways, such as age, class, income, leisure time activities and even psychological profiles or attitudes. The sheer bulk of available data on the subject of market segmentation entices major corporations utilizing mass media into the paradox of attempting to attract more and more *customers* for a particular product while directing the product's selling message to an ever narrowing audience. There is even talk now among media specialists of "subsegmentation strategies." Since advertising efficiency is a never ending quest for those spending millions and millions of dollars in advertising, this focus results in advertising directed to fewer and fewer *people* in an attempt to sell more and more of a particular product.

Those of us with our own small business are

fortunate to not have to go to such great lengths to find our *customers*. We usually know who they are and where they are. And like the ability to handle our *employees* one-on-one, the opportunity to deal with our *customers* on a one-to-one basis whenever possible is a significant advantage small companies have over large corporations, who must often set up *customer* relations departments or entire *customer* service divisions to handle problems, complaints or inquiries.

Small business owners who succeed not only listen to what their *customers* have to say, but more importantly, act on what they hear. Those entrepreneurs who often think they know better than their *customers* what is wanted will certainly fail.

A number of major corporations today are spending huge amounts of time and money implementing costly comprehensive *employee* motivation programs designed to make their companies more *"Customer* Oriented."

The very thought of high-powered corporate executives or highly paid management consultants acting as if the idea of putting *customers* first is some kind of "new found"' marketing approach or business success theory boggles the mind.

No business of any type can even exist without *customers.* This is no great revelation. The basic premise of survival in business is to provide a product or service which fulfills the needs and desires of the *people* who buy it from you.

It goes without saying that all *customers* pretty much want the same thing: a quality product or service at a fair price.

The right price is a powerful tool for achieving success but the men and women who succeed in taking their enterprises into the 1990's will not necessarily be those who offer their goods or assistance at the lowest price. Those entrepreneurs who recognize the opportunity when it arises to improve the quality of their business output by adding value to their products or services as well will be the ones who prevail in the long-run.

Look around, it's common knowledge that the quality of a tangible product influences buying behavior in America today. *People* are willing to pay more for better quality. The same is true of service. Only those companies which increase their *productivity* and provide the best possible service or the best quality product will attract enough *customers* to survive.

But attracting *customers* isn't enough. Too many

new business owners make it difficult for their *customers* to do business with them and their company suffers permanent damage in the form of lost *customers*. Just one lost *customer* can cost a company thousands of dollars in lost business.

New business owners of Professional Service firms such as lawyers and accountants refer to the *people* who purchase their services as *clients* rather than *customers* in order to suggest a more loyal relationship over a long period of time. Countless new business owners of all types will prevent their own success by treating their *customers* like *consumers* instead of like *clients*.

Ray Croc, most famous for founding the highly successful McDonald's Corporation, displayed a keen sense for recognizing the difference between *customers* and *clients* long before starting up his company which would revolutionize the food-service industry world-wide. In his autobiography, *Grinding It Out*, while describing the years he spent as a paper cup salesman for the Lily Tulip Company, he tells the following story:

> I peddled these cups all over Chicago. I sold lots of the smaller sizes to Italian pushcart vendors who filled them with flavored ice and sold one ounce for a penny, two ounces for two cents, and five ounces for a nickel.

> In 1930 I made a sale that not only gave Lily Tulip Cup Company a big boost in volume but also gave me an insight into a new direction for paper cup distribution. I was selling our little pleated soufflé cups to the Walgreen Drug Company, a Chicago firm that was just starting a period of tremendous expansion. They used these cups for serving sauces at their soda fountains. Observing the traffic at these soda fountains at noon, I perceived what I considered to be a golden opportunity. If they had our new Lily Tulip cups, they could sell malts and soft drinks to the overflow crowds. The Walgreens headquarters was at

Forty-third street and Bowen avenue at that time, and there was a company drugstore just down the street. I presented my pitch to the food-service man, a chap named McNamarra. He shook his head and threw up his hands at my suggestion.

"You're crazy or else you think I am," he protested. "I get the same fifteen cents for a malted if it's drunk at the counter, so why the hell should I pay a cent and a half for your cup and earn less?"

"You would increase your volume," I argued. "You could have a separate area at the counter where you would sell these things, put covers on them, and take them and the same vanilla wafers or crackers you serve with them at the fountain and drop them in a bag to take out."

Mac's face got redder than usual at that and he rolled his eyes toward heaven as if pleading to be delivered from this mad man.

"Listen, how can I possibly make a profit if I go to this extra expense? Then you want me to waste my clerks' time putting covers on drinks and stuffing them in bags? You are dreaming."

One day I said, "Mac, the only way in this world that you can increase your soda fountain volume is to sell to people who don't take up a stool. Look, I'll tell you what I'm going to do. I will give you 200 or 300 containers with covers, however many you need to try this for a month in your store down the street. Now most of your take out customers will be Walgreen employees from headquarters here, and you can conduct your own marketing survey on them and see how they like it. You get the cups free, so it's not going to cost you anything to try it."

Finally he agreed. I brought him the cups, and we set this thing up at one end of the soda fountain. It was a big success from the first day. It wasn't long before McNamarra was more excited about the idea of takeout than I was. We went in to see Fred Stoll, the Walgreen purchasing agent, and set up what was to be a highly satisfactory arrangement for both of us. The best part of it for me personally was that every time I saw a new Walgreens store going up it meant new business. This sort of multiplication was clearly the way to go. I spent less and less time chasing pushcart vendors around the West Side and more time cultivating large accounts where big turnover would automatically winch in sales in the thousands and hundreds of thousands.[1]

As stated in the previous chapter concerning *employees*, *people* are your most valuable asset. Those new business owners who do succeed will not fail to recognize *customers* and *clients* are *people* too.

If hardworking dedicated *employees* are the backbone of any successful business, loyal *customers* and *clients* are its lifeblood.

Getting *customers* is one thing; keeping them is another. Practically every successful business owner will agree that repeat business from current customers is the most critical element in any company's survival. With the whopping number of new business openings each year in virtually all industries or sectors of the economy, this quest is becoming more and more difficult to accomplish. There are only so many *people* to go around and they have more choices in today's marketplace than ever before.

That's competition and *customers* are what competition is all about. Those new business owners who will survive tomorrow are concentrating now on converting their present *customers* into long terms *clients*.

As mentioned in Chapter Five, *planning* your business is your most important job. How you plan to keep your *customers* coming back is the biggest part of that job.

You only have one chance to make a first impression with a new *customer*. In order to generate repeat business, you must create a satisfied *customer* the very first time. Why?

Because only a satisfied *customer* will likely become a repeat *customer*. Only after being satisfied repeatedly on a regular basis can a regular *customer* become a loyal *customer*. And loyal *customers* keep us in business because they want us to stay in business.

Tom Peters, author of *In Search of Excellence*, takes the concept of repeat business and *customer* loyalty to their maximum during a dissertation released on tape by the Nightingale-Conant Corporation titled *Creating the Lifetime Customer*.

"When you build a plant or purchase a big, new computer system, by both accounting conventions and also pretty much in the real world, the plant or the computer begins to depreciate on day number one. The antithesis of depreciation is obviously appreciation. And we don't think of an appreciating asset, but there is one. The appreciating asset is the well-served customer who becomes the most significant sustainer of the business, the lifetime customer."[2]

Whether we call them *customers*, *clients*, patrons, patients or whatever, it is essential to the success of our enterprise that we keep them coming back. Of course, obtaining new *customers* is vital, especially at first. But if you make it down the road to success, it will most likely be your old-line, long-time, repeat *customers* who will see you through the five-year barrier.

"Few people are successful unless a lot of other people want them to be."
-Charlie Bower

8

GROWTH,
SIZE
AND
SUCCESS

CHAPTER EIGHT

GROWTH, SIZE AND SUCCESS

"Success has made failures of many men."
-C. Adams

Some entrepreneurs wrongly assume the *size* of the company they open will somehow influence their *success*. They figure that being perceived as a large firm is the only way their enterprise can do big business.

They think that the number of *employees* hired and the amount of office, manufacturing or retail space leased is automatically connected to the number of *customers* they will attract or the amount of business they will reap.

These men and women often lose sight of the fact as expressed in Chapter Two that the size of a business is measured in one way and one way only…..by assets, and that this measurement is a *number* that doesn't even exist in real time.

Other new business upstarts feel that a company must be of a certain *size* in order to project a prosperous or favorable "image" to their *customers*. Large corporations are forced to invest millions of dollars in advertising designed to project a fabricated "image" or "personality" of themselves to the American public.

As a small business owner you are spared this burden of fabricating an artificial "image" since your enterprise presently contains an authentic, genuine "personality" of its own – you! Your honesty, confidence and enthusiasm, everything about you, is what projects the "image" of your company. How well you and your *employees* value your *customers* will determine your *success*, not the *size* of your organization or the scale of your physical operation.

Many entrepreneurs who fail get hooked on bigness for its own sake. You cannot grow your business bigger from the inside out or enlarge it simply by making it appear bigger.

New business owners who become fixated on *growth* usually get their companies into trouble. The history of business in America is filled with stories of promising young companies that appear on the scene from out of nowhere and experience a period of tremendous *growth*. They seem to enjoy instant *success* but then suddenly explode only to leave their founders bewildered, humbled and most often financially devastated.

Osborne Computer Corporation, once the darling of Silicon Valley, went from start-up to more than one hundred million dollars in sales in only a year and a half before winding up in bankruptcy court.

Worlds of Wonder, the high-tech toy company and producer of Laser Tag, which was the fastest selling toy in December of 1986, racking up well near one hundred million dollars in revenue, filed for protection under Chapter Eleven about a year later.

Pizza Time Theatres, Atari Corporation, People Express Airlines – the list goes on and on.

Some new business owners are driven by a desire to equal or top the *growth* of their competitors and frequently make the mistake of measuring their *success* by how fast they're growing. They concentrate on top-line growth and forget about everything else, like *profitability*, *productivity* or *planning*.

As expressed at the beginning of this book,

starting a business and staying in business are two different things. Successful, sound business *planning* does not necessarily mean a plan designed to achieve a rapid, astronomical *growth* rate.

It's how well your business grows that matters, not how fast it grows. A company's *growth*, although influenced in many ways by its internal structure and overall operation, is principally influenced by an outside force – *customer* demand.

Therefore, your first responsibility is to handle the volume of business you presently have. The role of *planning* for growth is to help prepare you to handle more business down the road. Careful *planning* today will insure the long life and prosperity of your business.

You will recall our discussion in Chapter Five

that *success* in business often depends on the ability to make the right decision at the right time. Managing *growth* is one of the trickiest parts of minding your own business. You should attempt to utilize your current resources to the fullest before expanding, but never be at *risk* of providing poor quality or poor service. Decisions in this area are crucial.

Make certain you grow your business and not your overhead. As your business grows, don't get carried away by the ease of hiring employees and overextend your fixed costs and expenses. Those who succeed only hire someone when their needs are busting out all over the place and they've already made enough BREAD to be able to afford it.

Don't hire *people* on iffy contracts or promises. Use temporary help to carry you through busy periods in order to increase *productivity* without runaway overhead.

Premature expansion can lead to excessive fixed overhead which chokes a newly founded enterprise that otherwise would have continued to survive at its present *size* and could be around to expand later.

This is not to say that *planning* for colossal *growth* is always wrong, Every company's situation is unique.

For example, Compaq Computer Corporation set a record at the time of its opening with thirty million dollars in funding for its venture before they even started up production. In 1983, the company's output went from two hundred machines to nine thousand and employment grew from one hundred *people* to six hundred. Today, Compaq is spearheading the challenge against IBM's leadership in the personal computer market. Experts have pointed out that without the massive funding in place, the astonishing rate of Compaq's early *growth* might well have broken its back and the company would have missed its chance in the market.

I am sure there are many other examples of pre-planned prosperity, but those business owners who let *customer* demand determine their company's rate of *growth* and thereby let their income determine their expenses, ordinarily have a higher *probability* of *success*.

As in the case with the Big Picture Opportunist, the-all-or-nothing *risk* is usually not worth the gamble.

With all due respect to Steve Jobs of Apple Computer, Fred Smith of Federal Express, Tom Monaghan of Domino's Pizza, Donald Trump and others whose enterprises have skyrocketed to fame and fortune, most people who own and operate successful, growing companies today are progressing at a much more modest pace. For every superstar who strikes it rich there are literally millions of us small business owners in charge of our own lives, following the American way and minding our own business.

Maybe someday you will make megabucks. I sure hope you do. But odds are you will have to break the *five year barrier* first and right now that's a fifty-fifty proposition for every new business owner.

Whether you produce a product, perform a service or both, try to make your output the very best. If you strive to be the best at what you do rather then the biggest, someday your company may become the biggest and the best.

In the meantime, staying mindful of the concepts

presented in this book concerning *Opportunity, Numbers, Words, Risk, Productivity, Employees, Customers* and *Success*, which are applicable to your situation as a new business owner, should help make minding your own business a lot easier ....and a lot more rewarding.

"He is well paid that is well satisfied."

-Shakespeare

BIBLIOGRAPHY

Bibliography

Chapter One

1. Roger Van Oech, A Kick in the Seat of the Pants, Harper and Row, 1986.

2. Ernest L. Boyer, College: The Undergraduate Experience in America, conducted by the Carnegie Foundation for the Advancement of Teaching, summarized in Time Magazine, November 10, 1986.

Chapter Two

1. Robert Heller, The Naked Manager, Great Britain, George Weidenfeld & Nicholson Ltd., 1972.

2. Victor Kiam, Going For It, New York, William Morrow & Company, Inc. 1986.

3. William W. Pyle and John Arch White, Fundamental Accounting Principles, Homewood, Illinois, Richard D. Irwin, Inc., 1966.

Chapter Three

1. Marshall McLuhon, Quentin Fiore, The Medium is the Message, New York, Bantam Books, Inc., 1967.

2. Alexander L. Sheff, Edna Ingalls, Mary S. Allen, How to Write Letters for All Occasions, New York, Doubleday & Company, Inc., 1961.

3. Robert Shurter, Written Communications in Business, New York, McGraw-Hill Book Company, 1971

4. Carl P. Wrighter, I Can Sell You Anything, New York, Ballantine Books, Inc., 1972.

5. Jerry Della Femina, From Those Wonderful Folks Who Brought You Pearl Harbor, New York, Simon and Shuster, Inc., 1970.

6. Daniel Robert White, The Official Lawyers Handbook, New York, Simon and Shuster, Inc., 1983.

7. Ibid, p. 179

8. Ibid, p. 188

Chapter Four

1. John E. Freund, Frank J. Williams, revised by Benjamin Perles and Charles Sullivan, Modern Business Statistics, Inglewood Cliffs, New Jersey, Prentice-Hall, Inc., 1969.

2. Peter Cohen, The Gospel According to the Harvard Business School, Doubleday and Company, Inc., 1973

3. Anthony Jay, Management and Machiavelli, New York, Holt, Rinehart and Winston, Inc., 1968.

Chapter Five

1. The President and Fellows of Harvard College, Harvard Business Review on Management, Harper and Row Publishers, Inc., 1975.

2. Ray Rowan, The Intuitive Manager, New York, Little Brown, Inc., 1986.

3. Fred Reinfield, How to Be a Winner at Chess, Fawcett Publications, Inc., 1954.

Chapter Six

1. George S. Odiorne, The Human Side of Management: Management by Integration and Control, D. C. Heath and Company, 1987.

2. Keith David, Ph.D., Human Relations at Work – The Dynamics of Organizational Behavior, McGraw Hill Book Company, 1967.

3. Editors and Experts of Boardroom Reports, The Book of Business Knowledge, Boardroom Reports, 1979.

*"People" performed by Barbara Streisand. Copyright held by songwriters Bob Merrill and Julie Styne.

Chapter Seven

1. Ray Kroc with Robert Anderson, Grinding It Out, Henry Regency Company, Chicago, 1977.

2. Tom Peters, Creating the Lifetime Customer, Nightingale-Conant Corp., 1987.